PUBLISHING INFORMATION

Ako Books is a New Zealand Playcentre Federation Social Enterprise Company in the business of producing educational books for parents, whānau and educators of young children since 1974. www.akobooks.co.nz

Established in the 1940s, Playcentre is a parent cooperative that offers quality early childhood education to over 10,000 New Zealand families across 500 Parent-Led Early Childhood Education Centres. www.playcentre.org.nz

First published in 2013

Published by:
Playcentre Publications Limited – Ako Books
www.akobooks.co.nz
0800 akobooks
email: info@akobooks.co.nz

Design by Beatnik

Printed by ROE Print Services Limited

Thank you to BJ Ball for supplying the paper for this book: This book is printed on ECO100 an environmentally responsible paper produced using Third Party certified 100% Post Consumer recycled Process Chlorine Free (PCF) pulp from responsible sources. Manufactured under the strict ISO14001 Environmental Management System and carries the internationally recognised Blue Angel, Nordic Swan, Austrian Environmental label and the NAPM recycled mark.

Thank you to Chris Parkin from http://smileifyouneedahand.wix.com/smile for the photo of Cathy Sheppard and to all the families around New Zealand who contributed the gorgeous photographs found throughout the book.

he pitopito kōrero // notes

INDEX
Rārangi Kaupapa

he pitopito kōrero // notes

FOREWORD

Messy Play is one of the great joys of early childhood. The freedom to play, experiment and explore is a simple treasure we can all give our children.

I have strong memories of my own childhood – lots of time spent outside, digging holes and making all sorts of mixtures. We would make mixtures in the kitchen cooked up for afternoon tea (some tasting better than others), mud pies in the sand pit, water with all sorts of flowers, leaves and dirt from the garden and wonderful mud slides down a slope on our lawn. Mum used to despair when she saw us getting the buckets out to make yet another stripe down the slope in the middle of an otherwise beautiful lawn.

What are some of your memories of Messy Play?

Playcentre has extended my repertoire for Messy Play, providing so many more varieties of texture. I love seeing the different looks on children's faces as they experiment – often initially tentative, curious, then looks full of sheer delight. Fun, laughter and learning abound.

This book draws on my many years working with young children. It combines classic recipes from our book 'Recipes for Play' with wonderful recipes from parents and educators from all around New Zealand.

Let's play!
Cathy Sheppard

WHY MESSY PLAY?

Messy Play is fun! Messy play is relaxing, allowing rhythmic movements of the whole body – great for relieving tension and frustration. Messy Play allows children and adults to express their feelings in a creative way. There is no right or wrong way, we can relax and enjoy the process. Patterns can be drawn and just as quickly erased.

Messy Play is a wonderful opportunity for learning:

- As a sensory learning experience, Messy Play offers a chance to enjoy and explore texture without restriction.

- Messy Play builds literacy skills, both in developing oral language and in developing the motor skills required for literacy and by drawing and writing as you play.

- Messy Play also helps to develop numeracy skills – dividing up quantities, creating and noticing patterns and shapes.

- There are so many opportunities for scientific exploration through Messy Play. How do different substances interact? How are different colours, textures and smells created?

- Messy Play is fantastic for building confidence and self-esteem – there's no right or wrong. The results are always original and different with no preset ideas.

- Messy Play offers lots of opportunities for building responsive and reciprocal relationships – joining in, sharing resources and ideas, laughing, chatting and making friends.

he pitopito kōrero // notes

THE VALUE OF MESSY PLAY IS IN THE DOING, NOT IN PRODUCING AN END PRODUCT...

Messy Play doesn't have to always be wet and dirty. There are other things around like sand, grass clippings, leaves and shredded paper.

Paint makes wonderful Messy Play. Try taking away the easels and using sponges, rollers, marbles and string. Put paper on the floor and encourage children to use their hands and feet. Try throwing paint sponges onto an outside wall/fence. What about allowing children to paint you?

Clay is great. Make a slurry. Many different cultures use clay to decorate bodies for different celebrations.

Add baking soda and vinegar into the mix and you have instant frothing fun.

Water also provides lots of opportunity for Messy Play, by adding bubbles, colour, or extending play in the sandpit.

Try adding different scents like eucalyptus and lavender for amazing smells.

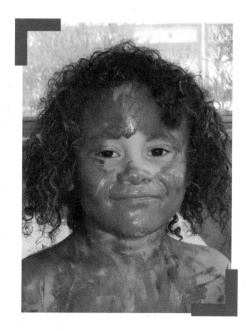

SETTING UP AND PLAYING

CHILDREN NEED:

- Clothing that they can relax and get mucky in
- Buckets of warm water and towels for washing hands and feet
- Enough space and enough medium to work with
- Time
- Low tables/troughs
- An adult working alongside them
- Music is also highly recommended – either singing or CDs. Classical music is great!

WHAT ADULTS CAN DO:

- Allow time and space for play
- Provide Messy Play often
- Provide a wide variety of Messy Play experiences and equipment like pipettes, hand mixers and wooden spoons
- Encourage and allow children to get dirty and messy. Providing them with clothes they can get dirty in means they can be unrestricted by aprons
- Relax and join in – get messy and lead by example
- Encourage discussion, experimenting, singing and music
- Help other children join in, find a space and participate
- Talk about the different textures – use words like slimy, soft, runny, warm, cold, lumpy, wet, thick, even 'dilatent'!
- Ask great open ended questions to encourage children's own thinking and learning processes
- Make clean up part of the activity and try not to rush – squirting the hose, a tub of warm water for washing containers – good clean fun

he pitopito kōrero // notes

SAFETY AND ALLERGY CONSIDERATIONS

Say Yes to Messy Play and No to nasty chemicals – a message from our friends at ecostore:

Having been Playcentre parents at Tutukaka, Malcolm and I both know the value of Messy Play and we love it, especially when there are a few simple safeguards in place around the types of materials we let our children play with.

Children love the look and feel of foam and bubbles, making dishwashing liquid an ideal material for Messy Play, but how many of us know what's actually in the dishwashing liquid we're using? It is easy to assume that if a product is available in supermarkets then it's safe to use, but this is not always the case.

With the recent rise in eczema and allergies many parents protect their children from ingesting things that might be harmful, however what goes on our skin is just as important as the food we eat. The skin is our largest organ and it can absorb chemicals that we come into contact with every day.

Not all chemicals are bad - water is a chemical after all, so it can be hard to know what's safe and what's not.

The chemicals listed below are often used in products like dishwashing liquid, as well as many body care products, including bubblebath and may be harmful to children's health. Look out for:

Cocamide DEA:

Cocamide DEA is commonly found in detergents and body care products. It acts as a foam stabiliser to boost foam and produce long lasting bubbles. Soaps and detergents don't actually need foam in order to clean.

Synthetic dyes – you could always add food colouring.

SLES (Sodium Laureth Sulphate)

For more on ingredients we think you should avoid come to ecostore.co.nz/ingredients

Melanie & Malcolm Rands – co-founders of ecostore

OTHER CONSIDERATIONS:

Fingerpaint, bubbles, paint, and soap-based recipes are very slippery. Put newspaper or towels on the floor if this becomes a problem.

Use rice flour in place of flour in playdough for those with gluten allergies. Use maize cornflour, rather than wheaten. The texture is better and means it is safe for all those with wheat allergies. If you don't need to cater for allergies, then wheaten cornflour does make better cooked fingerpaint.

We don't like playing with food. We do use flour and cornflour in quite a few recipes and we recommend that you keep special flour and cornflour that is not used for baking. Many people are conscious of this not only thinking of different cultural values, but also in not wishing to waste food.

Ready to get messy? Let's get started…

he pitopito kōrero // notes

FINGERPAINT
Te peita-ā-ringa

Basic fingerpaint can be cooked on the stove or whisked up using boiling water.

You can use tempera paint powder, food colouring, or dyes to colour. Paint gives the result an opaque colour; using food colouring or dye gives a translucent result.

Try experimenting with different smells and textures.

COOKED FINGERPAINT

INGREDIENTS:
2 cups Cornflour
5 cups Cold water

METHOD:

Mix the cornflour to a smooth paste with a little cold water in a large pot. Add 5 cups of cold water and stir over a low heat for about ten minutes until the mixture has thickened to a consistency that will pour slowly and keep its shape briefly when moulded or patterned with fingers.

Colour can be added while the fingerpaint is being cooked or mixed into the fingerpaint by children during play.

he pitopito kōrero // notes

UNCOOKED FINGERPAINT

INGREDIENTS:

2 cups Cornflour
1 cup Cold water
4-5 cups Boiling water
¼ cup Soap flakes (optional)

METHOD:

Whisk the cornflour and cold water together in a large bowl until all the cornflour is suspended. Pour in 4-5 cups of boiling water while stirring and beat until the mixture 'grabs'. Stir thoroughly until the mixture is smooth, thick and translucent.

Add the soap flakes if desired and keep stirring. If the mixture seems too thick, carefully add a little more water. The finished fingerpaint should pour slowly and keep its shape briefly when moulded or patterned with fingers. If the mixture doesn't 'grab', then simply add a bit more cornflour and microwave it for a couple of minutes.

Don't worry about lumpy fingerpaint, just think of it as another texture to explore!

Colour can be added to the bowl during the final stages of preparation or mixed into the fingerpaint by children during play.

SAFETY CONSIDERATIONS:

Let this mixture cool before putting it out for children as it's very hot when first made. Adding a little cold water when thinning it can help. Soap flakes may irritate if they get into the eyes, so remember to have some fresh warm water and towels on hand.

EASY TO CLEAN FINGERPAINT

The dishwashing liquid gives the fingerpaint a soapy-like feel, as well as making the fingerpaint easy to clean up and wash out of clothes.

INGREDIENTS:

1 cup Cornflour
½ cup Cold water
¼ cup Dishwashing liquid
2 cups Hot water
Colour and Essence

METHOD:

Mix cornflour, cold water, colour, essence and dishwashing liquid to form a thick paste like texture.

Quickly mix in the boiling water to form a glossy paste.

Thanks to Rachelle Lang, Greenpark Playcentre

CORNFLOUR AND TALCUM POWDER FINGERPAINT

This fingerpaint is very smooth and slippery with the consistency of thick handcream and a distinctive soapy smell.

INGREDIENTS:

1 ½ cups Cornflour
1-1½ litres Boiling water
1 ½ cups Soap flakes
½ cup Talcum powder

METHOD:

Mix the cornflour to a smooth paste with a little cold water in a large pot. Add the boiling water and stir until the mixture 'grabs'. It may be necessary to cook the mixture at this stage until it is translucent and thick. Add soap flakes and talcum powder and stir thoroughly. It will be a little runny when first made, but will set as it cools.

SAFETY CONSIDERATIONS:

Talcum powder should not be breathed in so be careful when adding. Soap flakes may irritate if they get into the eyes, so remember to have some fresh warm water and towels on hand.

he pitopito kōrero // notes

TEMPERA POWDER FINGERPAINT

INGREDIENTS:

Tempera Paint Powder
Water

METHOD:

Make up packets of tempera paint powder using hot water. The powder will mix quickly into a thick smooth paint that can be successfully used as fingerpaint.

CLAY FINGERPAINT

INGREDIENTS:

Clay (dry or damp)
Water
Dishwashing liquid

METHOD:

Break the clay down by hammering dry clay to dust or by breaking damp 'plastic' clay into small pieces. Add water until the mixture has the required smooth, runny consistency. A few drops of dishwashing liquid will change the consistency into a more flowing liquid. Experiment to see which you prefer.

he pitopito kōrero // notes

CORNFLOUR GLOOP

Gloop is an amazing substance and fascinating to play with. The scientific word to describe Gloop is 'dilatent' – if you apply pressure to Gloop it goes solid; releasing the pressure makes it a liquid. It also dries on clothing and brushes of easily as a powder!

INGREDIENTS:

2 cups Cornflour
1 cup Cold water

METHOD:

Pour the cornflour into a bowl. Add the cold water and mix, adding a little more water if needed.

Use a little food colouring to colour the mixture, or make it white and provide colours alongside for children to add themselves.

WET TO DRY GLOOP

INGREDIENTS:

4-5 cups Cornflour
Jug of water
Powdered dye

METHOD:

In a trough put a cup of cornflour in front of each child. Let them explore the texture with their hands. Slowly pour a little water in at a time encouraging children to mix it with their hands. The mixture changes from a thick moulding consistency to drizzling off the hand and finally becomes a water play activity. After adding a little water the powered dye can be sprinkled in. Use different colours and watch them blend!

Thanks to Kyla Rigby, Kumeu Village Kindergarten

he pitopito kōrero // notes

CORNFLOUR GLOOP MOUNTAIN

This is a variation on Gloop, which also enables children to experience the multiple forms of Gloop.
Great for scientific exploration and developing working theories.

INGREDIENTS:

4-5 cups Cornflour
Cold water to mix

METHOD:

Make a mountain of cornflour in the middle of a small trough, high sided tray, or low sided bowl. Put some water around the outside making a moat. Encourage children to mix it using their hands, adding a little more water at a time as needed. Adding too much water turns it into a milk-like consistency and you'll need to add more cornflour.

he pitopito kōrero // notes

RAINBOW GLOOP

INGREDIENTS:

Cornflour
Food colouring/Dye

METHOD:

You may or may not wish to dilute the colouring with water as we love the intensity of the coloured Gloop you get with an undiluted colour source.

Add liquid colouring in small amounts to cornflour until you find the perfect point where it is liquid when left to run and solid under pressure.

Make 4-6 different colours and pour them separately into a water trough or large tray.

To make rainbows – pick up and pour/drip one colour into a pool of a different colour. Because of the consistency, the colours stay side by side. It actually takes quite a bit of effort to mix them into new colours.

Thanks to Anna McDonald, Auckland Playcentres Association

he pitopito kōrero // notes

PAVEMENT PAINT

INGREDIENTS:
½ cup Cornflour
½ tsp Powered dye
½ cup Water

METHOD:
Combine all ingredients and stir until you have a smooth consistency.
Make different colours and invite children to paint it onto concrete. The
mixture goes on wet like paint and dries like chalk with vibrant colour.

Thanks to Kyla Rigby, Kumeu Village Kindergarten

ICE CHALK

INGREDIENTS:
Coloured Gloop
Water
Ice cube trays

METHOD:
Once everyone has finished playing with the coloured Gloop, if it is cleanish (no grass, dirt, etc) carefully scoop it up into a bowl, add ½ cup cold water and mix to a liquid. Pour this into ice trays and freeze. Once frozen, you have Ice Chalk. This is great to use on black paper as it looks like melted water on the page and once it dries it makes a wonderfully vibrant picture.

Even better, if there is any chalk left leave it in a bowl to melt and you once again have Gloop. And so the cycle continues.

Thanks to Rachelle Lang, Greenpark Playcentre

he pitopito kōrero // notes

GLOW IN THE DARK GLOOP

INGREDIENTS:
Cornflour
Tonic Water to mix to consistency
1 UV Blacklight bulb

METHOD:

Blackout room with binbags, install UV bulb, combine ingredients and play in the dark!

Thanks to the team at Awatere Playcentre

he pitopito kōrero // notes

OTHER INTERESTING SENSATIONS
He Mahi Whakamīharo Kē

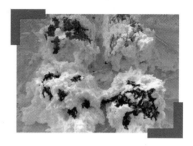

SOAP FLAKE FOAM

INGREDIENTS:
1-2 cups Soap flakes
Hot water

METHOD:
Pour 1-2 cups of soap flakes into a bowl and add hot water until the soap flakes are completely covered and the water is just above their level in the bowl. Beat the mixture until the soap flakes dissolve and the mixture has the consistency of canned shaving foam.

Try putting drops of colour on top of the foam and not mixing. Invite children to feel the texture of the foam and experiment with mixing the colours together.

SAFETY CONSIDERATIONS:
Soap flakes may irritate if they get into the eyes, so remember to have some fresh warm water and towels on hand.

he pitopito kōrero // notes

SOAP FLAKE GEL

INGREDIENTS:

2 cups Soap flakes
3 cups Hot water
Food colouring for colour if desired

METHOD:

Pour 2 cups of soap flakes into a bowl and add 3 cups of hot water. Mix until the soap flakes have dissolved and leave for about an hour until the solution has set. Alternatively make the gel the night before it is required. This mixture is translucent and thick and keeps well.

he pitopito kōrero // notes

SAND MOUSSE

Children love mixing sand and water. This recipe creates a totally different texture, making a lovely soft, fluffy mixture. Try and limit the amount of water added. If children add too much water, add more sand.

INGREDIENTS:
1 cup Dishwashing liquid
Lots of sand
Water to mix

METHOD:
Put lots of sand in a low trough or clam shell. Invite children to add the dishwashing liquid and water to mix. Mix and add more sand or water as needed.

Thanks to Ruth Vaughan, Hutt Playcentre Association

SLIME

There are so many options for playing with soap flakes and water. This recipe makes an amazing substance we like to call SLIME.

INGREDIENTS:
1 cup Soap flakes
4 cups Hot water

METHOD:
Dissolve the soap flakes in the hot water in a large bowl or bucket. Add colour if desired and leave to stand for at least an hour. The resulting play material will froth up if beaten, pours easily and is extremely slimy to the touch. It keeps very well.

he pitopito kōrero // notes

SOAP PAINT FOR THE BATH

This recipe is great fun for bathtime at home and also on session in tubs.

INGREDIENTS:

¼ cup Non toxic handsoap, bodywash or
shampoo. Dishwashing liquid is fine
¼ cup Cornflour
1 tsp Food colouring

METHOD:

Mix the liquid soap with the cornflour, then food colouring. If too thin for your liking, add extra cornflour; if too thick, add extra soap or water.

You can divide the flour soap mix into different containers and make a few different colours.

Let the bathtime fun begin!

Thanks to Andrea Morgan, Johnsonville Playcentre

he pitopito kōrero // notes

DRY MESSY PLAY

This mixture is great for rainy days/inside play, and is fantastic for children who don't like other types of Messy Play as it doesn't stick to their hands. The mixture can be recycled and kept in a container from session to session.

INGREDIENTS:

Ordinary flour or rice flour
Tempera paint powder

METHOD:

Put flour mixed with tempera paint powder in a trough. Add hands, wooden spoons, sieves, cups, whisks – any tools you would use for water play work great.

NOTE:

Adding water makes a fantastic witch's potion, a very different consistency to gloop or fingerpaint. However, cleaning up afterwards is very difficult! If you don't want water added to it, don't put it anywhere near the water trough, especially with adventuresome 4 year olds around!

Remember flour and water makes glue.

he pitopito kōrero // notes

BASIC PLAYDOUGH

There are so many fantastic playdough recipes. This one is a favourite as it's the easiest to make with children. In this recipe the boiling water is added last, so children can help right up to this point. Making playdough together is a wonderful opportunity to explore numeracy and science. You can work with groups of children, providing them all with a bowl and wooden spoon for mixing and measuring equipment. When making this with groups of children, don't be too fussy on exact quantities – whatever you end up with will be fun!

INGREDIENTS:

3 cups flour
1 ½ cups salt
6 tsps Cream of tartar
3 Tbsps Cooking oil
3 cups Boiling water

METHOD:

Mix the dry ingredients and cooking oil together, then add boiling water. If working with groups of children, divide quantities amongst the bowls. Stir well until the mixture leaves the sides of the bowl. Add more flour if the mixture seems to sticky, then turn out and knead.

he pitopito kōrero // notes

GLUTEN FREE PLAYDOUGH

INGREDIENTS:

1 cup Rice flour
1 cup Maize Cornflour
1 cup Salt
4 tsps Cream of tartar
2 tsps Vegetable oil
2 cups Hot water

METHOD:

Combine all ingredients in a pot and cook over a low heat stirring as you go until the mixture leaves the sides of the pot and reaches a dough like consistency. Turn out and knead.

he pitopito kōrero // notes

USING OLD PLAYDOUGH FOR MAGIC POTIONS

Old Playdough makes for fantastic Messy Play!

Put pieces of it in small containers and spread these around a table with an ice-block stick or similar in each.

In the middle of the table have containers of sand, bark bits, flour, water, leaves.

Encourage children to add what they wish, mixing and stirring.

Providing vinegar and baking soda adds an extra bit of excitement!

WATER AND ICE
Te wai me te tio

ICE MAGIC

In winter, freeze a shallow layer about 3cm deep in your water trough outside over night. Or if you live in a warmer part of the country freeze shallow trays of water. You can also do this with big blocks of ice.

INGREDIENTS:
Food colouring diluted in palettes
Pipettes
Salt

METHOD:
Children can use pipettes to drop food colouring on the ice, sprinkle salt in areas to melt and stick sheets together.

Thanks to the team at Awatere Playcentre

he pitopito kōrero // notes

BUBBLES
Ngā mirumiru

BASIC BUBBLES

For instant bubble mixture, use dishwashing liquid, diluted with a little water if desired.

INGREDIENTS:
9 Tbsp Dishwashing liquid
1 Tbsp Glycerine

METHOD:
Stir together carefully so that the mixture doesn't froth up too much. The glycerine will make the bubbles stronger and last longer. Tip the mixture into a large flat dish to allow a variety of bubble wands to be used.

FOR HOME-MADE BUBBLE WANDS, TRY THE FOLLOWING:

- Wire or plastic twisty ties bent into the required shape.

- Shapes cut from the lids of plastic containers.

- Cotton reels or other plastic tubes such as wool cones.

- Plastic rings held with a spring clip peg.

- Your fingers.

he pitopito kōrero // notes

GIANT BUBBLES

INGREDIENTS:

12 cups Water
1 cup Dishwashing liquid
1 cup Cornflour
2 tsps Baking powder

METHOD:

Measure all ingredients into a large rimmed bucket or bowl and mix gently. Leave to settle for about an hour.

Use big round wands – the bigger the better or make your own using wire/old wire coat hangers.

Dip and wave! Huge bubbles to chase around the garden!

Thanks to Jane Dowd, Spring Creek Playcentre

he pitopito kōrero // notes

MORE GIANT BUBBLES

INGREDIENTS:

1 cup Detergent
4 tbsp Glycerine
10 cups Water
(needs more in warm weather)

BUBBLES AND STRAWS

Give children wide containers of bubble mix coloured with a bit of food colouring and a straw. Encourage children to blow lots of bubbles up in the water.

Prints can be taken by putting a piece of paper over the top of the bubbles.

What else can you do with a straw and bubbles? Can you get a bubble on the table and blow it up bigger with a straw inside?

Thanks to Liz Neill, Hutt Playcentre Association

he pitopito kōrero // notes

PAINT
Te Mahi Peita

Paint makes wonderful Messy Play. Try taking away the easels and using sponges, rollers, marbles or string. Put paper on the floor and use your hands and feet. Try throwing paint sponges onto an outside wall/fence. Paint bodies, add water and mix.

NOTE:
For children into mixing large quantities of paint, try using very runny cooked fingerpaint of different colours as an alternative. It's a little cheaper!

TRY PUFF PAINT:
Mix equal parts salt and self-raising flour then add enough water so that the mixture can be painted with a brush onto paper. When finished microwave for 1 minute and enjoy the puffy result.

he pitopito kōrero // notes

EVOLVING PAINT - MESSY PLAY ACTIVITY

This uses paint on a large piece of plywood or similar, with rollers and squeegees. The children spread the paint around first on the ply with the squeegees and rollers to cover it...

Then they can get their bodies involved in the action and then on to paper.

Thanks to Emma Pritchard, Morningside Playcentre

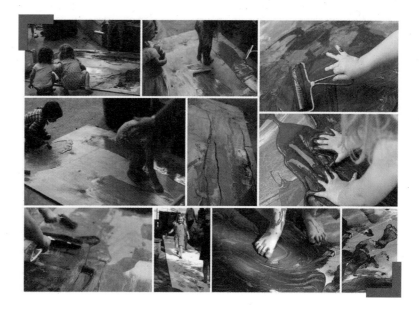

he pitopito kōrero // notes

MARBLING

INGREDIENTS:

2 or 3 colours of food colouring
Vegetable oil or baby oil
Tray
Water
Pipettes
Matchsticks
Paper

METHOD:

Place a very shallow layer of water in the tray – just enough to cover the bottom.

Mix oil and food colouring (approx 2 tablespoons of each) in a container until roughly combined. Remember that as this is oil and food colouring, they won't combine completely.

Use pipettes to place drops of the oil/food colouring mixture onto the water, then use fingers or matchsticks to swirl and combine. Place paper softly to float on the surface, then remove when you can see the image coming through.

Thanks to the team at Awatere Playcentre

he pitopito kōrero // notes

CLAY
Te uku

Clay provides so many opportunities for Messy Play, especially by adding water.

RECONSTITUTING OLD CLAY

Clay that is old and dry can be reconstituted by soaking it in a bucket of water. As it softens, cut it into smaller pieces and keep dipping it in water as you gradually work it into a usable consistency.

If it's totally bone dry, crush it up with a hammer, then dump it into a bucket of water. The clay will settle, then you can scoop off the water from the top. The sludge can then be poured through an old cotton pillowcase or similar to drain off the excess water and then you can begin to work the clay into a more usable consistency. Great Messy Play, and great for the environment and budget too.

CLAY SLURRY

Put lumps of soft clay in a trough with water, then squeeze and squish it until you have made a wonderful, thick clay slurry. This can be kept in an airtight container and used for many sessions, adding more water if it dries out.

he pitopito kōrero // notes

WOOL
Te wūru

FELTING ROCKS

INGREDIENTS:

Some found stones from the river or beach
Dishwashing liquid
Warm water
Wool batting/roving

METHOD:

Fill a bowl with warm water and soap – make the water as warm as you possibly can. Get your stones and wind wool roving around them. You can use different colours and thicknesses. Dip your stones in the warm water and start to rub them gently. This process takes a while but can take on many different forms with children sinking their stones in the water, rubbing, patting, or stroking the stones. If children don't like getting their hands soapy, you can put the stones in a plastic bag and felt them by rubbing the plastic bag. The stones are done when the roving has felted up and feels firm with no gaps. Although anything goes really..

Thanks to Sian Hannagan, near the Taieri River

he pitopito kōrero // notes

PAPER
Te pepa

SHREDDED PAPER

Get a pile of newspapers and put on some nice classical music. Walk around while tearing the paper with your hands to the beat of the music. Very quickly there will be a lovely pile of shredded paper which can then be played in. This paper can then be used for papier maché, or for making recycled paper.

PAPIER MACHÉ

Papier Maché creations can be made by layering strips of paper with a flour and water paste onto a base such as a balloon, or by moulding pulped paper.

PAPER SCULPTURES

Tear old newspapers into small pieces. Place in hot water to soak for half an hour or so. Add colour or texture (with leaves etc) if desired. Use a whisk or stick blender, or the children's willing hands to create "mush". Use the mush to make shapes and sculptures.

Thanks to Anna McDonald, Auckland Playcentres Association

he pitopito kōrero // notes

BONUS FOAM FUN!

FOAM ERUPTIONS

This is a great science experiment with 'wow factor'. The baking soda reacts with the lemon juice/citric acid releasing carbon-dioxide as a by product. The bubbly gas released produces super foam from the hand soap. The super foam is then cold to the touch – do you know why?

INGREDIENTS:

¼ cup Clear liquid hand soap
¾ cup Warm water
2 Tbsp Baking soda
2 Tbsp Citric acid, or lemon juice (try using both and experimenting to see what works best)
Food colouring

METHOD:

Set out small containers in a deep basin or water trough. Add clear hand soap and warm water to each container and invite the children to mix to create soapy water. Add a few drops of food colouring to each one.

Invite children to add spoonfuls of baking soda to each bowl of soapy water and mix it in – it should become gooey. The children can then add spoonfuls of citric acid (or lemon juice). As soon as the citric acid/lemon juice hits the baking soda/soapy water combination, it will create a very light, airy, fluffy foam.

Set out small spoons or sticks for mixing. The more the children mix in the citric acid, the lighter, fluffier and bigger foam they'll get!

Tip out all of the containers into a large container – get stuck in with hands and mix for some extra foamy fun!

he pitopito kōrero // notes

CLOUD FOAM

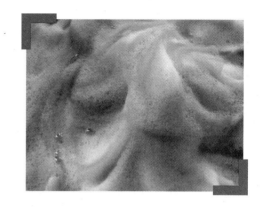

INGREDIENTS:

2 Tbsp of Dishwashing liquid
¼ cup water
An electric mixer
Food colouring

METHOD:

In a bowl, add dishwashing liquid and water. Add food colouring to the mix if desired. Mix on the highest possible setting for 1-2 minutes.

Your foam should be able to form stiff peaks that hold their shape.

Scoop it out into your container and repeat as necessary until you have the desired amount of foam!

he pitopito kōrero // notes

RAINBOW FOAM DOUGH

INGREDIENTS:
A batch of Soap Flake Foam from page 21
Cornflour
Colour

METHOD:
Foam Dough has two ingredients in a roughly one to one ratio – cornflour and Soap Flake Foam. Put Soap Flake Foam in individual containers for each colour you want to create and start by colouring the Soap Flake Foam with food colouring.

Slowly add cornflour to each colour and stir until it starts looking a little doughy. Keep the dough on the wet side so it is fluffier. The more cornflour you add, the drier the dough.

It will be a fluffy puffy fun cloud!

he pitopito kōrero // notes

AND LAST BUT NOT LEAST MUD…

There's nothing better than a decent sized, well watered mud puddle. Either naturally formed or dig your own. Can be used with plastic animals, vehicles and whole body immersion. Not to mention delicious mud pies!

Thanks to Silo Park Playcentre

he pitopito kōrero // notes

ESSENTIAL INGREDIENTS LIST:

Here's a basic list of Messy Play ingredients to always have on hand.
Please remember to keep baking/cooking ingredients separate from
Messy Play ingredients.

Flour and Rice Flour
Cornflour
Baking Soda
Vinegar
Citric Acid
Cooking Oil
Glycerine
Salt
Clay
Soap Flakes

ecostore Dishwashing Liquid
Food colouring
Tempera paint
Dye
Essential Oils and Essence for
lovely smells
Sand
Dirt
Leaves
Add Children and Mix

he pitopito kōrero // notes

he pitopito kōrero // notes

he pitopito kōrero // notes